D1242571

in SCARLET AND BLUE

The Story of Military Uniforms in America

Written and illustrated by
DIRK GRINGHUIS

THE DIAL PRESS

NEW YORK

To
TED HASKELL
Military historian, collector,
bagpiper, and Little War
General without peer.

Special thanks to:

Colonel Frederick P. Todd
Director, West Point Museum

Lt. Col. Tom Tryon, U.S.A.F.R.

Master Sergeant William E. Brovold
U.S. Army Recruiting Service

MANUFACTURED IN THE UNITED STATES OF AMERICA

CONTENTS

YESTERDAY'S UNIFORMS

See the flash of gold braid on scarlet or blue, waving horse-hair plumes above gleaming helmets, silver lace, shaggy bearskin caps, polished leather shakos. Here are the parade uniforms of yesterday and today—the dress of the soldier when he is not at war.

Pomp is for peacetime. Combat troops always need comfort, but it has only been in the last seventy years that real comfort and camouflage have been used in uniforms. In past centuries bright uniforms were worn on the battlefield as well as on parade. The range of weapons was so limited and smoke clouds were so great that the soldiers usually couldn't even see the bright colors of the enemies' coats. American soldiers were about the only ones allowed to enjoy the comfort of combat uniforms. This was because of the rugged country over which they had to fight.

Uniforms began a little over three hundred years ago. In feudal times great nobles and barons rode out with gentlemen bodyguards. These retainers, as the bodyguards were called, wore the colors and badges of their lords. By the fifteenth century, though, the power of the nobles gave way to the power of the kings. The lords still paid for the clothes their men wore, but the display was now designed to lend brilliance to the crown.

16TH CENTURY
YEOMAN
OF THE GUARD

PIKEMAN

MUSKETEER

In 1458 Matthias Corvinus of Hungary sent out invitations to his coronation. On the invitation appeared a woodcut of a man on horseback. "A little pattern of a man" it was called. Guests and nobles were ordered to outfit their retainers in this single style.

They arrived, uniformly dressed. The age of uniforms had begun.

There were four main reasons for wearing uniforms. First was recognition—being able to tell friend from foe as well as separating the different regiments. Formerly, colored scarves were worn, but too often this led to trickery through the simple exchange of colors. Swapping uniforms was a more difficult matter.

Second, a line or column of uniformed troops made a most impressive sight in the eyes of the enemy. The brilliant coats, gleaming helmets, and polished boots could also turn a slender, pink-cheeked boy into a dashing adventurer, so uniforms became effective as recruiting posters.

As armies changed from roving bands of paid fighters (mercenaries) into regular standing units, a third reason appeared. A spirit was developing, a new spirit of pride, pride not only in uniform but in the regiment. Pride of comrades, of leaders, and of country. The army calls it *esprit de corps* (espree d'core).

There was also an economical reason. To clothe an army required many bolts of cloth, and buying all the bolts in a single color was cheaper.

Military uniforms always follow civilian dress of the times, but at the same time a soldier, marine, or sailor must look like a fighting man. He must look taller, stronger, and braver. Plumes added height to the headgear. Coats were designed to broaden the shoulder and puff out the chest. Belts nipped in the waist. Tight breeches or leggings slimmed the leg and rounded the calf.

Peacetime uniforms were usually the battle dress of the previous war with added trimmings. During a war caps were jammed down for comfort, plumes and lace were discarded. Afterward, in the following peace, the cry went up to "smarten up the army," and battle dress turned into parade dress. Dress parades were common in winter camps and during times of relative quiet until after our Civil War.

Styles were usually set by victorious armies whose uniforms were then copied by other armies of the world. After the French victories in the 1850's, for example, most of the world's armies adopted French-style uniforms. Even the U.S. Army uniforms of the Civil War included the French-styled *képi*, or cap, and the long overcoat with cape.

As for colors, the French blue, British red, Austrian white, all appear to be accidents of history. Whoever started the story about red coats being worn to hide bloodstains never saw service. The fact is that blue and red were less likely to fade.

The changes in Army, Navy, Marine, and later Air Force uniforms usually reflect the influences of utility, decoration, and the styles of other times and other countries.

PARADE   COMBAT

Early Colonial Army

It is necessary that uniforms be sturdy enough to stand up under hard wear and at the same time be smart. This, ultimately, meant two uniforms, parade dress and service or battle dress. Battle dress in early colonial days, however, was often designed by the men themselves. In combat or in special surroundings, such as forest warfare in early America, troops simplified and adapted their only uniform. Coats were shortened, caps were cut down to avoid overhanging branches. More comfortable garments were finally approved and used. But the changes were slow in coming. Until the 1840's in America soldiers wore dress uniforms in battle. Their muzzle-loading weapons had to be loaded standing up, and men were not trained to take cover; thus they didn't get their uniforms dirty. It was not until breech-loading weapons allowed the men to reload lying down and under cover that dress uniforms in battle were ruled out in favor of so-called fatigue uniforms.

For the discussion of uniforms we will say that the Army had two major branches, foot and mounted troops. Each had special uniforms designed for his particular job Generally, foot soldiers wore longer coats and loose-fitting breeches for easy walking. Mounted troops wore shorter coats for easier mounting, and their breeches were designed to fit more tightly under high boots to protect the men from saddle chafe.

The first regular foot regiment in the American colonies was a British unit sent by King Charles II in 1677 to put down a rebellion in Virginia. Commanded by Colonel Herbert Jeffery it was called "Jeffery's Regiment of Foot."

The uniform was made up of a long red coat with blue lining, breeches, shirt, neckpiece, and shoes. Hats were wide-brimmed and had a flat crown. A red cap was furnished also. Breeches and stockings probably matched the blue of the coat linings. Cost of the uniform was deducted from the man's pay.

Officers wore coats of their own choosing and of various colors, trimmed with as much lace as they could afford. Some wore the uniform of their former regular regiment in England, the yellow of the Maritime Regiment, the scarlet and blue of the First Guards, or simply red coats. Weapons carried by the men were muskets—matchlock or flintlock, or long-handled spears called pikes, swords and sword belts, cartridge boxes or bandoliers, and hatchets.

JEFFERY'S REGIMENT
OF FOOT   1677

FRENCH AND INDIAN WAR
1754-1763

During the long struggle between the French and English for possession of North America a new style of British uniform appeared. The colonial troops, who usually dressed as woodsmen, wore *this* style uniform when serving with a regular regiment such as the Royal Americans. Typical of these uniforms were those worn by the 44th and 48th Regiments of Foot under General Braddock.

Based on civilian clothing, the red coats were square-skirted and long, nearly to the knee. Lower corners were folded and fastened back, the beginning of the tail coat. Waistcoats, breeches, and high-buttoned gaiters completed the uniform. Coat lapels and cuffs, called facings, carried the colors of the regiment. A waist belt or shoulder belt held a cartridge box, a short sword, or a bayonet. A pack and canteen were also held by shoulder belts.

Hats were no longer wide-brimmed as in early colonial days. By the end of the seventeenth century they were cocked in several styles, one of which was the *tricorne*. This was a three-cornered hat with a decoration on the left side called a cockade, and it became standard military headgear.

Grenadier companies wore special headgear. Because these men needed both hands free to throw grenades, they had to sling their muskets over their shoulders. The tricorne, of course, got in the way and was knocked askew or completely off, so a brimless grenadier cap was designed. Later it grew very tall and pointed, faced with a regimental plate in various colors and bearing the initials GR for George Rex, King George.

One of the most exciting and courageous regiments ever to serve in America was the Royal Highland Regiment of Foot called the Black Watch. They wore militarized Highland dress, a short scarlet jacket trimmed with regimental lace on front and sleeves, blue facings, a scarlet waistcoat, and the traditional Highland kilt. The tartan pattern in the kilt was a dark green and gray-blue with a red stripe added for full dress and for grenadiers. This tartan became known as the Black Watch tartan or plaid. For full dress a long-belted plaid was also worn. In front of the kilt hung the goat skin purse or *sporran*. Stockings were checkered and reached to the knee. On their heads they wore the blue bonnet with a red pompon and a strip of bearskin on the left side. Grenadiers wore tall cloth caps edged with fur. For field work or boat duty, kilts were replaced with canvas breeches and blue leggings. Sometimes the kilt was also worn with leggings. Their weapons were the musket, bayonet, broadsword, dirk, and Scots' pistol.

The same blue Scots' bonnet was also preferred headgear by the famous company of rangers commanded by Major Robert Rogers of Northwest Passage fame. These men were light foot or scouts, expert marksmen trained in forest warfare. They wore a dark green, fringed hunting shirt over fringed Indian leggings and Indian moccasins. Besides the light musket, they carried a tomahawk and sometimes a bayonet. Knapsacks, often of fur, were worn high between the shoulders. Canteens were cloth-covered.

Major Rogers is pictured wearing a light infantryman's cap, a cut down tricorn like a small grenadier's cap, with steel crown and chains for protection. Across his right shoulder he wears a broad belt, or baldric, with brilliant colored Indian beadwork.

AMERICAN REVOLUTION
1775-1783

When General George Washington became Commander-in-Chief of the Continental Army, there were few "American" uniforms of any kind. Most volunteers wore ordinary clothes or the fur cap and the hunting shirt of the woodsman. Because of the great expense of fitting out an army, the hunting shirt became the first distinct uniform of the American soldier. For nearly a year the only regulation uniforms were those worn by state militia and provided by the states themselves. Others fought in homespun or buckskin.

In 1776 four regiments of Continental light dragoons were raised. These men were hand-picked for excellent horsemanship and unquestioning loyalty. When uniforms were available, they were of a distinctive cut, and each regiment had its own colors. Coats were short, and breeches were made of buff leather with knee-length boots. A broad white shoulder belt held the cartridge box, and the heavy sabre hung from a waist belt. Pistols were mounted on the saddle. Short muskets called carbines were carried when available. Caps, made of heavy leather with a short visor, were rounded at the top and carried plumes of horsehair or feathers.

British uniforms, except for the red coats, were very similar in cut to those of the American troops. Both armies wore their hair larded down for neatness, powdered white, and tied in a pigtail. Some wore a little pigtail turned up and tied with a leather strap, leaving a knot of hair below.

Certain British regiments had distinctive uniforms. The British-hired German troops, mercenaries of the Hessian and Brunswick regiments, wore dark blue coats, buff breeches, and black leggings. Officers wore the gorget, a half-moon of metal worn at the throat, like that worn by British officers. Grenadiers in the field sometimes wore striped overalls made from tenting material. These were a most practical garment and became standard for most armies by 1780. Brunswick *dragoons,* mercenaries with fierce mustaches, wore the heavy equipment of the European dragoon. Coats were light blue with yellow facings. Boots were huge and heavily reinforced about the knee to stand the shock of mounted charge and hand-to-hand combat. Jaegers (hunters) served as rangers. They wore green coats and waistcoats with white metal buttons, scarlet lapels, collars, and cuffs. Their breeches were buff leather. These men carried fine German rifles and straight hunting swords.

BRITISH TROOPER
WEARING CUIRASS

GRENADIER

BRUNSWICK DRAGOON

JAEGER

Army

Then, in 1776, Congress authorized General Washington to raise a full army and equip it with uniforms. But cloth was scarce and full uniforms were few until America became allied with France.

During most of the war soldiers were expected to wear the black tricorn with cockade, a brown, blue, or natural wool coat, a buff waistcoat, breeches, and leggings. Most wore what they could find.

Uniforms were grouped by states in 1779 and lapel facings told from which state they came. White was for New England, buff for New York and New Jersey, blue for Georgia, etc.

The cavalry, traditionally divided into two groups, heavy and light, had their own uniforms. The heavy cavalry was formed on the image of earlier mounted knights in full armor and riding powerful horses, while the light cavalry originated with the knights' more lightly armed attendants. The former was of little use in the rough and wooded terrain of America's eastern seaboard, but light cavalrymen, fighting mounted and armed with swords, pistols, and lances, were needed to act as scouts, couriers, patrols, military police, and honor guards. Another division of the cavalry were the dragoons. Named after a gun, the old "dragon," they also fought mounted, carrying muskets as well as swords and pistols and riding heavier horses. Dismounted, they fought as infantrymen.

AMERICAN
LIGHT
DRAGOONS

Navy

The first regulations for naval uniforms seem to have been issued in 1776. They called for a blue cutaway coat with red lapels, stand-up collar, flat gold buttons, blue breeches, and a red vest trimmed with gold.

Sailors wore a dark blue cloth jacket with a double row of buttons, white waistcoat, a black neckerchief, blue breeches over gray stockings, and square-toed, buckled shoes. The breeches were covered to the knee with a white canvas skirt or apron, like fishermen wore. The hat was soft and black with a narrow brim.

British seamen wore much the same uniform except that some pictures show them wearing a cocked hat and striped shirt.

In 1777 officers' regulations changed. A captain then wore a dark blue coat with white lapels from shoulder to waist. The collar was standing and blue. There were three buttons on each cuff and pocket flap. Breeches, vest, and stockings were white, the vest decorated with gold lace. On the right shoulder, a gold epaulet was worn.

Marines

Marines are soldiers of the sea and a part of the Navy. Continental Marine officers wore a green cutaway faced with white. Officers' buttons were silver, enlisted men's pewter, and all had the fouled anchor design. Breeches and vests were white with green trim. Men wore green shirts, white wool jackets, light-colored breeches, and wool stockings. Both officers and men wore black gaiters. Headdress was a cocked hat for officers and a round hat bound in white for the men. All ranks kept their hair powdered. Officers wore a silver epaulet on the right shoulder.

WAR OF 1812-1814

At the end of the eighteenth century, following the War for Independence, the Regular Army in America was reduced to under a hundred men. The common militia attempted to curb the Indians on the wide frontiers and failed. Finally, after 1791, a regular force was raised under the command of General Anthony Wayne. Called Wayne's Legion, it was a force of mixed arms, infantry, cavalry, and artillery. To impress the Indians, they wore a smart uniform on parade of dark blue with red facings and waistcoat. White crossbelts, kept clean with pipe clay, held their equipment. Officers wore cocked hats with a feather; the men wore leather caps trimmed with a bearskin roach. Cockades held a feather. Service dress, along the war trails, was the fringed buckskin jacket.

WAYNE'S LEGION
1795

BRITISH 1800

Army

At the beginning of the nineteenth century civilian costume had changed and so, too, had uniforms. The clumsy tricorn which had hung on for one hundred years disappeared. Officers exchanged their cocked hat for one that was folded in two and worn fore-and-aft with points in back and front, or square-rig with points at either side. Short breeches with knee gaiters of fourteen or fifteen buttons were replaced with practical trousers and calf-high gaiters. Uniforms now took on the French style as worn by Napoleon's powerful armies.

One change, important for comfort, was the shortening of the coat into the coatee, with which Napoleon outfitted his troops before invading Russia. Pantaloons also were worn. French foot soldiers' headgear became the shako, a tall felt or leather cap with a front plate of metal, circled with cords, and topped with a pompon or plumes. The elite guard, crack regiments, followed grenadier tradition and donned the imposing bearskin cap.

In America the new war with England called for sudden measures. Uniforms, if they could be called uniforms, were hastily issued of gray, brown, or other neutral colors. Some men were still wearing the overalls of Wayne's Legion, recently disbanded after the Indian wars on the Ohio frontier.

But the uniform style was French and made up of a coatee and ankle-length pantaloons worn over short leggings or spatterdashes. In 1813 foot soldiers adopted British-style leather shakos. High in front, they were similar to French shakos, but they had a flap behind to protect the neck. The tasseled cord, circling the cap, was fastened on the left with a leather cockade and a brass eagle with pompon.

By 1815 supply began to catch up with demand, and the American army took on a more martial appearance. At the battle of Chippewa, victorious American troops appeared with a new shako and gray uniforms with white crossbelts.

This is the uniform that eventually became the symbol of victory. Adopted for cadets at West Point, it still exists, almost unchanged. The white crossbelts are worn for drill.

Navy

After the Revolution the American Navy disappeared until 1798, when Congress ordered the building of six new frigates. The short blue jacket and soft hat were still worn upon the return of the Navy. But instead of skirt, breeches, and stockings, the men wore long pantaloons. They also kept the knotted black neckerchief.

1812 saw further changes. Blue coats reached below the waist and trousers had bell-shaped bottoms. The wide bottoms were possibly designed to be rolled up when swabbing decks. The hat was narrow-brimmed and shiny with a tall, flat crown, something like a formal top hat of today.

By 1813 regulations allowed officers, as well as the men, to wear pantaloons instead of breeches.

During the war British and American uniforms were so much alike that cases actually occurred when foe was mistaken for friend. Only close examination could tell that British buttons showed anchors while the American buttons had the eagle and anchor on them.

Marines

In 1798 the President approved the establishment of the first United States Marines. Uniform regulations called for a blue cloth jacket, lapelled, faced and edged in red, with a red belt and cuffs. Collar, shoulder strap, and vest were also red over blue wool overalls with red seams. Buttons were the same as on the navy jacket. Hats were brimmed and turned up on the left side with a leather cockade and trimmed in yellow. White linen overalls were issued for summer wear.

By 1804 the swallow-tailed coat, buttoned to the neck and with a high standing collar, replaced the cutaway. Officers' coats were double-breasted with two rows of eight buttons. Buttonholes were laced and brought to a point at the center. Vest and pantaloons were white. Officers wore a cocked hat with scarlet plume and tassels. Summer hats were round. A scarlet sash, tied outside the coat, and black knee-high boots were added for full dress.

Enlisted men wore a shako with a red plush plume in front, a single-breasted swallow-tailed coat faced in yellow, white cloth pantaloons, and black calf-high gaiters.

In 1805 officers were ordered to wear white crossbelts with gilt plates in front. Men's gaiters were extended to reach to the knee.

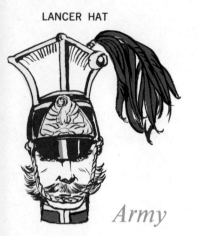

LANCER HAT

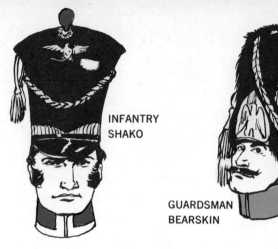

INFANTRY
SHAKO

GUARDSMAN
BEARSKIN

PEACE 1814-1845

Army

HUSSAR
BUSBY

With the end of the Napoleonic Wars, uniforms approached their most extravagant era in Europe. Among the most colorful of all were those worn by the cavalry. Light horse cavalrymen wore uniforms patterned after the original Hungarian hussars, a fanciful and barbaric costume worn by all hussars until the age of mechanization. Caps were of fur and called busbys, copied after the Turkish hat, with a lining which was turned out and hung down in a fold.

Lancers throughout Europe adopted the style of the Polish light horse. The Polish cap was even more unusual, very high with a square top made of cane and covered with cloth the color of the uniform facings. A brass plate adorned the front with a great plume high above. This was part of the uniform of the famous Light Brigade of Balaclava.

Elite infantry wore the tall bearskin cap, or the shako, which also grew in height and began to flare at the top.

By 1830 uniforms became so fanciful that they served little purpose except for parade. Tunics grew so tight that cavalry

28

could hardly use their sword arms. Breeches had to fit without a wrinkle. Helmets sprouted bearskin crests so tall that they were hard to keep on in a high wind, impossible in a charge. Bell-topped shakos became top heavy with plumes, badges, and cords. Even saddles were huge with scarlet and gold cloth, even leopard skins. In England the cost of equipping a single officer in a crack regiment ran close to $2,000.

But in America these brilliant uniforms were found only in the state volunteer companies. Independent, private organizations, they differed from the standing militia (civilians subject to call for service) by being trained and uniformed at their own expense. One of the oldest was the Ancient and Honorable Artillery Company formed in Boston in 1638 and still in existence. These topnotch regiments were the forerunners of the American National Guard. Company names were the Grays, the Blues, Hussars, Dragoons, Fencibles, etc.

The most exotic foot units were the Zouaves. Raised first by the French in the 1830's, they were dressed in the style of Algerian mountain tribesmen. The costume was a short, blue, embroidered jacket, baggy red trousers, and white leggings. On their heads they wore red fezzes with a tassel. The first company of American Zouaves, raised in 1859, specialized in complicated and brilliant drill exhibitions, performed at a quickstep.

In the 1830's, during the Seminole War, the first campaign or fatigue uniforms were worn. By 1845, during the Mexican War, campaign dress for enlisted men was a short jacket, long trousers, and a soft-topped cap with a visor, much like a yachtsman's cap today. Officers wore frock coats, single-breasted, with the same caps as the men.

ZOUAVE

29

SAILOR

MARINE

Navy

In 1835 sailors wore a dark blue cloth jacket, dark blue trousers, white shirt, and a large blue collar trimmed with white. Hats were black with two ribbons behind.

Officer's dress changed little except that lapels were now the same color as the coat. Trousers were long and blue with a gold stripe.

Marines

By 1833 the blue uniforms had changed again to the green of colonial times. Trousers were gray in winter, white in summer. Officers wore a cocked hat with a plume.

In 1839, however, the corps changed back to blue coats. Officers coats were double-breasted with a standing collar decorated in gold lace. Trousers were dark blue with a 1¾-inch red stripe. Black boots were worn under the trousers and a crimson sash with gold-fringed ends was tied around the waist and knotted on the left side. Their head covering was a black beaver hat with red cock feathers.

Enlisted men during the Mexican War wore blue coats buttoned high at the throat, white crossbelts, and shakos. Campaign dress was gray, with hats soft like those of the Army.

CIVIL WAR 1860-1865

Army

Infantry played the major role in the American Civil War, but outfitting them was slow as usual. Although both North and South rushed to arms, it was six months before either side was ready to take the field.

Uniforms for the U.S. Army from 1861 to the end of the war were almost unchanged. Enlisted men wore dark blue four-button sack coats with turndown collars, a dark blue cap or kepi (French), and light blue trousers as fatigue dress. Frock coats and felt hats were also worn.

Officers wore the frock coat with shoulder straps denoting rank. Trousers were dark blue with a gold seam welt or cord the color of their branch of service. These colors were: cavalry, yellow; infantry, light blue; artillery, red; etc.

Headgear was either a black felt hat or kepi. All officers wore a sash passed twice around the waist, tied on the left. General officers' sashes were buff; surgeons', green; all others, crimson. A black leather sword belt with two slings and a hook held the sword. These were worn over the sash.

Overcoats for officers were dark blue, but the enlisted men had sky-blue overcoats with a cape, French-style.

Besides colored facings to denote branch of service, devices also appeared on the cap front—bugles for infantry, crossed sabres for cavalry, and crossed cannons for artillery. Regimental numbers appeared within or above the cap device.

Confederate uniforms were gray, the coats double-breasted for both officers and men. Caps were gray kepis but many preferred slouch hats.

As the war stretched on, many soldiers replaced parts of their uniforms with more comfortable attire, such as cotton shirts for summer, a blanket slung over the shoulders instead of bulky knapsacks, and a short jacket to replace the coat.

Zouaves fought, at first, wearing brilliant uniforms. However, they finally realized that the bright colors made them easy targets and gradually changed into more somber clothing.

Navy

Throughout the Civil War Federal officers had both dress and service uniforms. Both coats were dark blue, double-breasted, with roll collar and dark blue trousers. Full dress required a cocked hat and gold epaulets, while black leather belts had a yellow gilt belt plate with a wreath, a spread eagle, an anchor, and thirteen stars. Belts were worn over the coat.

Federal sailors wore dark blue uniforms consisting of a woolen shirt, trousers, and a flat-topped round cap with a ribbon, a black silk neckerchief, and black shoes. Warm-weather uniforms were white duck.

Confederate uniforms were steel gray. Officers wore double-breasted frock coats with two rows of gilt buttons and gray trousers and cap.

Sailors wore gray jackets, trousers, and a black hat.

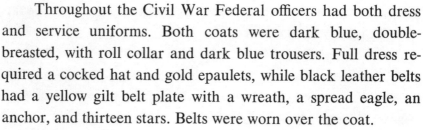

Marines

U.S. Marine officers wore double-breasted frock coats. Trousers were light blue in winter, white in summer. Headdress for field officers and the commandant was the chapeau, a flat-sided hat worn fore-and-aft. Other officers wore a dark blue cap with a visor and a shield of the U.S. with the letter M. A pompon of gold net two inches high was perched on top of the cap.

Men in full dress wore a double-breasted frock coat with two rows of seven buttons, sky-blue trousers, and a cap like the officers with a red pompon. Service coats were single-breasted with seven buttons. Overcoats were gray-blue, single-breasted, with seven buttons and a cape.

From the Civil War until the Spanish-American War, Marine service uniforms were a dark blue blouse and cap and sky-blue trousers. Enlisted men's coats were plain. Officers had rows of black across the front. Officers' swords were the slightly curved scimitar type with a white grip and straight cross guard.

PEACE 1872-1898

Army

Between 1874 and 1880 Army uniforms changed again. At first a shorter shako replaced the kepi as a standard headpiece. Then, as before, the successes of a European army imposed a new style on the world's armies. This time the style was set by the Prussians after the Franco-Prussian War. Originally used in Denmark, the spiked helmet or *Pickelhaube* was adopted by the Prussians, then by England, Russia, and the United States. Mounted officers wore it with the plume. Custer's famous 7th Cavalry of Indian War fame wore it with their dress uniform. The plumes matched the color of the shoulder knots denoting the service. Full-dress coats were double-breasted and epaulets were replaced with colored shoulder knots.

Dismounted, officers wore the helmet also, but replaced the plume with the brass spike. Sashes no longer were used and the sword belt became gold with silk colors. Trousers were light blue with a 1½-inch gold stripe down the seam.

Enlisted men wore the single-breasted frock coat with helmets either plumed or spiked. Mounted officers used the sabre, dismounted officers the straight two-edged sword.

SPANISH-AMERICAN WAR

Army

During the short war with Spain another uniform period began. Khaki (from the Hindu meaning dust) turned up as the official color for regular service uniforms as more accurate rifles made camouflage more important than good looks. The wide-brimmed campaign hat formerly used by western frontier troops became popular.

Theodore Roosevelt raised the Roughriders (First Volunteer Cavalry) as a mounted unit ready for action in Cuba. Uniforms were khaki and had a blouse instead of a coat, leggings to the knee, and a slouch hat bearing the crossed sabres of the cavalry.

After the war, uniforms underwent still another change. The helmet and chapeau completely disappeared and were replaced with the beginnings of our present-day visored cap. This uniform was kept until the beginning of World War I.

Navy

After the Civil War, full-dress uniforms for officers became the double-breasted swallow-tailed coat of dark blue worn with dark blue trousers with gold stripes and a cocked hat. Gold epaulets and a gold-striped dark blue sword belt completed the uniform. The service uniform, also adopted for general wear, included a cap, plain dark blue trousers, and a single-breasted sack coat. This coat was braided in black around the collar, down the front, around the bottom, and up the back seam. Insignia of rank was worn on the collar and cuffs.

A white service uniform was worn in hot weather. This had a white-topped cap, single-breasted coat with five gilt buttons, and white trousers. Sword belts were worn under the coat.

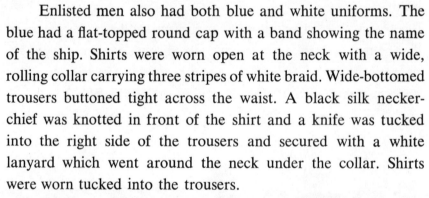

Enlisted men also had both blue and white uniforms. The blue had a flat-topped round cap with a band showing the name of the ship. Shirts were worn open at the neck with a wide, rolling collar carrying three stripes of white braid. Wide-bottomed trousers buttoned tight across the waist. A black silk neckerchief was knotted in front of the shirt and a knife was tucked into the right side of the trousers and secured with a white lanyard which went around the neck under the collar. Shirts were worn tucked into the trousers.

Summer uniforms had a white turned-up cap, a white shirt worn outside, black neck scarf, and white trousers.

Marines

From the Spanish-American War through World War I, there were several kinds of uniforms worn by the Marine Corps: full dress, undress, white undress, summer field, and winter field.

Officers in full dress wore a dark blue cap with a black sloping visor, a gold chin strap, and a gold MC device. Coats were dark blue double-breasted frocks with a standing collar. General officers wore dark blue trousers with a gold stripe; staff officers, a scarlet stripe; others had sky-blue trousers with a ½-inch scarlet stripe.

Undress uniforms consisted of a dark blue visored cap and a dark blue single-breasted sack coat with five gilt buttons down the center. Rank was worn on shoulder straps. Trousers were dark blue with a black stripe for generals, a scarlet stripe for staff officers; others wore sky-blue trousers with scarlet. White undress followed the same pattern.

Field uniforms for summer had either the same visored cap in khaki or the wide-brimmed campaign hat with a crown that was dented in four places. On the front was the Marine Corps insignia showing the globe with the Western Hemisphere resting on a fouled anchor and topped by a spread eagle. Hats also had a red cord with acorn ends.

Coats were khaki sack with a standing collar and four patch- and buttoned-pockets. Breeches were khaki without a stripe and were worn with leather puttees and tan shoes. Mounted officers wore boots. Winter uniforms were the same except for the color which was forest green.

Enlisted men's dress uniform had the dark blue cap with leather chin strap and the Corps emblem in gilt. Coats were dark blue single-breasted with seven gilt buttons. Coats were now piped around all edges in scarlet. Trousers were sky-blue with a one-inch scarlet stripe. White trousers and a white cap cover were also worn. Waist belts, worn outside the coat, were white with gilt plate.

WORLD WAR I

Army

Only service uniforms were worn during hostilities, and there was little change in design. Uniform colors were olive drab or khaki, a return to the practical "work-camouflage" principle occurring in wartime. Officers wore the letters U. S. on the collar. Enlisted men wore a bronze button on either side, the left carrying the letters U. S., the right, the device (emblem) of the arm of service. Favorite headgear was the wide-brimmed, soft-crowned campaign hat worn cowboy style. Another cap appeared also. Called the overseas cap, it was patterned after the Scots Glengarry bonnet, a soft, visorless and brimless cap that fitted the head. In France the men wore steel helmets that had a round top with a slightly sloping brim and a leather strap which passed under the chin. Officers overseas wore sword belts with a strap running across the right shoulder. Officers wore riding breeches and boots or puttees of leather. Enlisted men wore wrapped woolen puttees originating with the British Army in India. A miserable arrangement, puttees had the unhappy habit of coming unwrapped. Enlisted men in the cavalry wore knee-high laced boots.

Army Air Corps

With the adoption of the airplane for warfare, a new service arm was added to the Army. At first Army aviators were part of the Signal Corps, but later they became a separate corps. Uniforms were like those of the Army with the exception of a silver embroidered double-winged shield on the left breast. All aviators were officers. Enlisted men who worked on the planes wore an Air Corps insignia on the right sleeve below the shoulder.

Navy

Again, all uniforms were service. Enlisted men still wore the same dress as in the Spanish-American War, except shirts were worn outside the trousers and knives no longer were carried. White hats could now be worn with both blues and whites.

Shortly after the war the English-styled service coat was adopted by officers. Double-breasted with open lapels and turn-down collar, they were worn with white shirts and a black four-in-hand tie.

WORLD WAR II

Changes in World War II were mostly for added utility and comfort in the field. A combat dress of green herringbone twill appeared as the first uniform ever designed for fatigue and combat wear only. Collars were worn open and the clumsy puttee was replaced by the legging and the combat boot for infantry.

With mechanization and the end of the horse cavalry, troopers exchanged riding breeches and high boots for the more comfortable trouser and low boot.

Caps were the barracks-type, round and topped with a forepiece bearing the Army eagle in gold on the front. The garrison cap (overseas type) was also worn.

The dress uniform was blue, and olive drab was worn in the field. Coats were at first single-breasted with four buttons and four buttoned pockets. Rank appeared on shoulders and shirt collars, branch of service on lapels.

Later, the short jacket appeared. It was first copied from the American lumberjack by the British. Later, the style was worn by General Eisenhower, and eventually became known as the Eisenhower jacket. This short, tight-waisted blouse was worn through World War II and up to about 1960. British soldiers still wear it.

Field dress was much the same for officers and men. During combat even insignia was hidden to foil enemy snipers. Helmets had changed from the flat type of World War I into a rounder, closer-fitting helmet offering better protection. These helmets have a padded liner made of fibre to fit inside the steel helmet and absorb shocks. Liners alone are worn for drill and noncombat conditions because they are much lighter in weight. Summer service uniforms were sun tan cotton.

Air Corps, Navy, and Marine uniforms were much the same as today.

UNIFORMS TODAY

Jeffery's Foot, the first regular regiment in America, had the cost of their uniforms deducted from their small pay. Today's recruit faces a happier prospect. Upon enlistment he is issued personal clothing effects free. They are his own property and he is also paid $4.20 monthly extra for clothing maintenance for three years. The allowance is then raised to $5.40 to replace worn out items. His allotment is worth around $350 and includes two service uniforms of dark green, replacing olive drab, five sets of summer khakis, and three sets of green fatigue or work uniforms. These are worn with the Ridgeway cap, named after General Matthew Ridgeway. The recruit also receives two pairs of combat boots, one pair of oxfords, five pairs of cushion-soled socks, three pairs of dress socks in black, one garrison cap, one service cap, a black web belt with brass buckle, a raincoat, an overcoat and liner, and leather gloves with wool liners.

Other special clothing is loaned to him for special duties or combat training. These include the M-1 or M-14 rifle, cartridge belt and scabbard, helmet with liner, gas mask, entrenching tool, canteen and cup, mess kit, field pack with harness, cargo pack for extras, blanket, shelter half (pup tent), field jacket, shirt, trousers of olive green, overshoes, insulated boots, parka, work gloves, etc.

41

MODERN
INFANTRYMAN

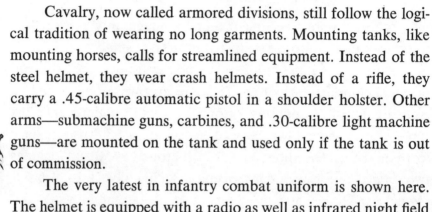

Cavalry, now called armored divisions, still follow the logical tradition of wearing no long garments. Mounting tanks, like mounting horses, calls for streamlined equipment. Instead of the steel helmet, they wear crash helmets. Instead of a rifle, they carry a .45-calibre automatic pistol in a shoulder holster. Other arms—submachine guns, carbines, and .30-calibre light machine guns—are mounted on the tank and used only if the tank is out of commission.

The very latest in infantry combat uniform is shown here. The helmet is equipped with a radio as well as infrared night field glasses. Under the jacket he is wearing body armor. His weapon is a new automatic rifle.

Army Air Force

After World War II the Air Corps became a separate branch called the Air Force. They have their own Air Force Academy just as the Army has West Point, the Navy, Annapolis.

Today's Air Force wears a blue service uniform and blue summer uniform. Dress uniforms are also blue, worn with a blue shirt and dark blue tie. Formal wear requires a white shirt and black bow tie. Buttons and cap devices are silver. Caps are either the round-topped barracks-type or the flat, brimless flight cap. Blue overcoats are worn with gray mufflers and gloves.

AIR FORCE

Navy

Naval officers' uniforms are almost unchanged since World War II. Service uniforms are blue for winter, white for summer. Work uniforms are khaki. All are styled as single-breasted sack coats with three buttons. Full dress is dark blue double-breasted with a white-topped cap.

Enlisted men still wear the wide-collared shirt, scarf, and wide-bottomed trousers. Winter uniforms are blue, summer are white. Both the round blue and the white caps are worn. Work uniforms are blue dungarees.

Marine and Navy Air Corps

Flyers wear forest green winter uniforms, khaki for service dress and for working dress.

Marines

The only change in uniforms since World War II is that coats and trousers are both of a slightly darker shade of blue.

For three hundred years uniforms have been constantly changing. At this very moment changes are still going on. The dash and glitter, the tall bearskins, busbys, plumed helmets are seen only on those milita company color guard in America that retain their full-dress uniforms for parades. But even on service uniforms, the small tokens of centuries remain. Feudal badges have become shoulder patches. Medals are tiny bars of colored silk. And the *esprit de corps,* the pride in a top outfit, lives on.

We in America are building our traditions through the pride of free men—men who believe in their country and in the comrades who shared in the making of it.

IDENTIFICATION CHART OF HEADGEA

	ARMY	NAVY	MARINES
AMERICAN REVOLUTION			
WAR OF 1812			
MEXICAN WAR			
CIVIL WAR			
SPANISH-AMERICAN WAR			
WORLD WAR I			
WORLD WAR II			